D0757606

MIGHTY MACHINES

TANKER TRUCKS

by Wendy Strobel Dieker

AMICUS | AMICUS INK

tank

manhole

Look for these words and pictures as you read.

tape

sign

Here comes a tanker truck.

What is inside?

See the tank?
It holds liquids.
It takes water to a fire.

tank

A tanker hauls dry goods too.
It holds sugar.
It goes to a candy factory.

See the manhole?

It opens.

Milk goes in the tank.

manhole

See the tape?
It is on the sides.
It is on the back. It helps
other cars see the truck.

tape

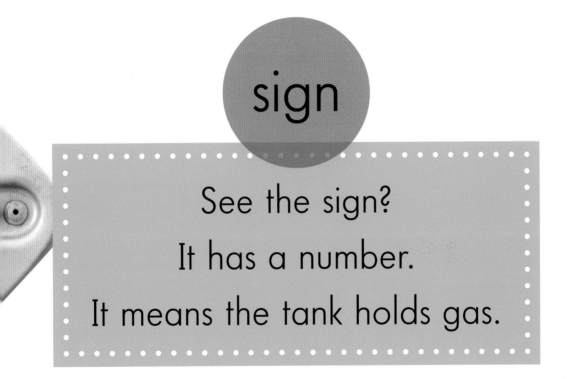

sign

See the sign?

It has a number.

It means the tank holds gas.

A hose hooks up to the tank.

It empties the tank.

Time to get the next load.

See the tank?
It holds liquids.
It takes water to a fire.

tank

See the manhole?
It opens.
Milk goes in the tank.

manhole

tank

manhole

Did you find?

tape

sign

See the tape?
It is on the sides.
It is on the back. It helps
other cars see the truck.

tape

1203

sign

See the sign?
It has a number.
It means the tank holds gas.

Spot is published by Amicus and Amicus Ink
P.O. Box 1329, Mankato, MN 56002
www.amicuspublishing.us

Library of Congress Cataloging-in-Publication Data
Names: Dieker, Wendy Strobel, author.
Title: Tanker trucks / by Wendy Strobel Dieker.
Description: Mankato, Minnesota : Amicus, [2019] | Series:
Spot. Mighty machines | Audience: K to Grade 3.
Identifiers: LCCN 2017033356 (print) | LCCN 2017055724 (
  (ebook) | ISBN 9781681514581 (pdf) | ISBN 9781681513768
  (library binding) | ISBN 9781681522968 (pbk.)
Subjects: LCSH: Tank trucks--Juvenile literature. | CYAC: Tank
  trucks. Classification: LCC TL230.15 (ebook) |
  LCC TL230.15.D545 2019 (print) | DDC 629.224--dc23
LC record available at https://lccn.loc.gov/2017033356

Printed in China

HC 10 9 8 7 6 5 4 3 2 1
PB 10 9 8 7 6 5 4 3 2 1

To my favorite mighty machine
drivers, Big Jerr and Smoke 'em
Joe —WSD

Rebecca Glaser, editor
Deb Miner, series designer
Aubrey Harper, book designer
Holly Young, photo researcher

Photos by Dreamstime/Taina
Sohlman, cover, 16; iStock/
ryasick, 1, Grafissimo, 3,
DarthArt, 4–5, kozmoat98, 6–7,
WendellandCarolyn 14–15;
Shutterstock/Pavel L Photo and
Video, 8–9, iidea studio, 10–11,
iofoto, 12–13

TANKER TRUCKS